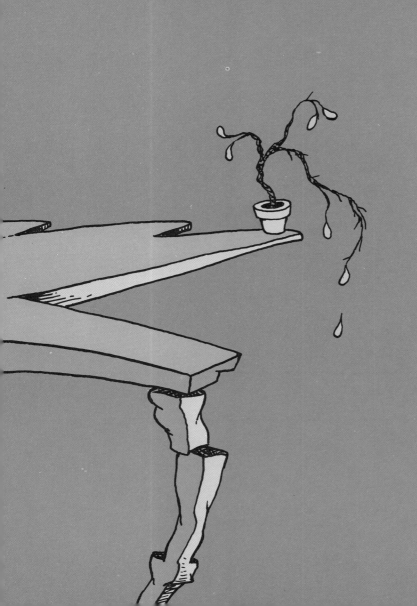

Did
I
Ever
Tell You
How Lucky
You Are ?

Did I Ever Tell You How Lucky You Are?

By Dr. Seuss

COLLINS

6 8 10 9 7 5

ISBN 0 00 171610 7 (paperback)
ISBN 0 00 171609 3 (hardback)

© 1973 by Dr. Seuss Enterprises, L.P.
All Rights Reserved
Published by arrangement with Random House Inc.,
New York, USA
First published in the UK 1974
First published in this edition 1990 by
HarperCollins*Children's Books,*
a division of HarperCollins*Publishers* Ltd

Printed and bound in Hong Kong

This Book,
With Love,
is for
Phyllis
the Jackson

When I was quite young
and quite small for my size,
I met an old man in the Desert of Drize.
And he sang me a song I will never forget.
At least, well, I haven't forgotten it yet.

He sat in a terribly prickly place.
But he sang with a sunny sweet smile on his face:

When you think things are bad,
when you feel sour and blue,
when you start to get mad...
you should do what *I* do!

Just tell yourself, Duckie,
you're really quite lucky!
Some people are much more...
oh, ever so much more...
oh, muchly much-much more
unlucky than you!

Be glad you don't work on the Bunglebung Bridge
that they're building across Boober Bay at Bumm Ridge.

It's a troublesome world. All the people who're in it
are troubled with troubles almost every minute.
You ought to be thankful, a whole heaping lot,
for the places and people you're lucky you're *not!*

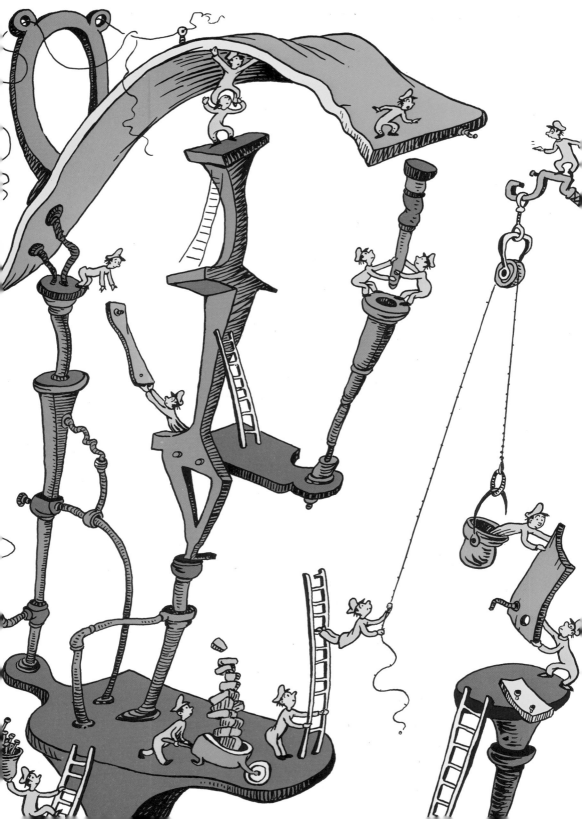

Just suppose, for example,
you lived in Ga-Zayt
and got caught in that traffic
on Zayt Highway Eight!

Or suppose,
just for instance,
you lived in Ga-Zair
with your bedroom up here
and your bathroom up THERE!

Suppose, just suppose, you were poor Herbie Hart,
who has taken his Throm-dim-bu-lator apart!
He *never* will get it together, I'm sure.
He never will know if the Gick or the Goor
fits into the Skrux or the Snux or the Snoor.
Yes, Duckie, you're lucky you're not Herbie Hart
who has taken his Throm-dim-bu-lator apart.

Think they work *you* too hard...?
Think of poor Ali Sard!
He has to mow grass in his uncle's back yard
and it's quick-growing grass
and it grows as he mows it.
The faster he mows it, the faster he grows it.
And all that his stingy old uncle will pay
for his shoving that mower around in that hay
is the piffulous pay of two Dooklas a day.
And Ali can't *live* on such piffulous pay!

SO...

He has to paint flagpoles
on Sundays in Grooz.
How lucky you are
you don't live in *his* shoes!

And poor Mr. Bix!
Every morning at six,
poor Mr. Bix has his Borfin to fix!

It doesn't seem fair. It just doesn't seem right,
but his Borfin just seems to go shlump every night.
It shlumps in a heap, sadly needing repair.
Bix figures it's due to the local night air.

It takes him all day to *un*-shlump it.
And then...
the night air comes back
and it shlumps once again!

So don't *you* feel blue. Don't get down in the dumps.
You're lucky you don't have a Borfin that shlumps.

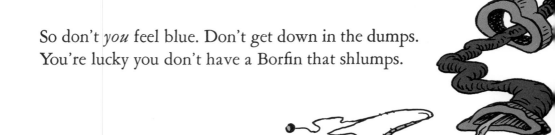

And, while we are at it, consider the Schlottz,
the Crumple-horn, Web-footed, Green-bearded Schlottz,
whose tail is entailed with un-solvable knots.

If *he* isn't muchly
more worse off than you,
I'll eat my umbrella.
That's just what I'll do.

And you're lucky, indeed, you don't ride on a camel.
To ride on a camel, you sit on a wamel.
A wamel, you know, is a sort of a saddle
held on by a button that's known as a faddle.
And, boy! If your old wamel-faddle gets loose,
I'm telling you, Duckie, you're gone like a goose.

And poor Mr. Potter,
T-crosser,
I-dotter.
He has to cross *t*'s
and he has to dot *i*'s
in an I-and-T factory
out in Van Nuys!

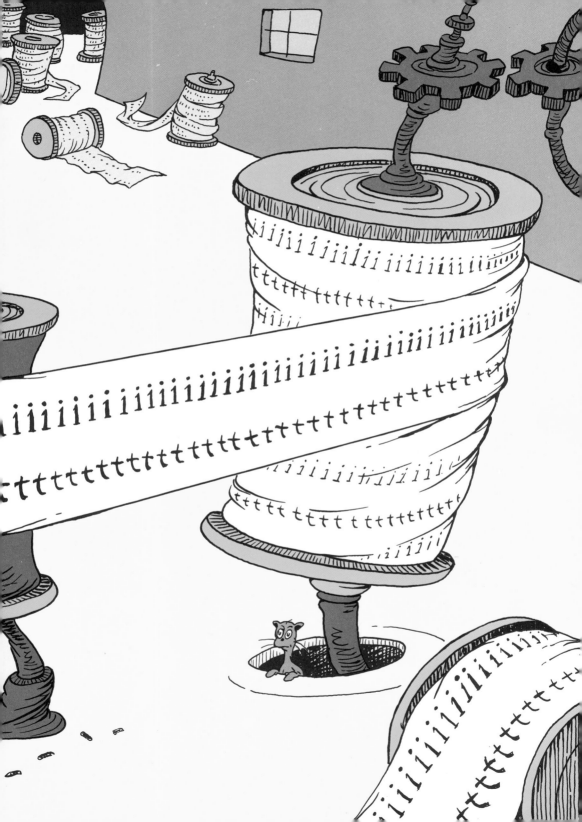

Oh, the jobs people work at!
Out west, near Hawtch-Hawtch,
there's a Hawtch-Hawtcher Bee-Watcher.
His job is to watch...
is to keep both his eyes on the lazy town bee.
A bee that is watched will work harder, you see.

Well...he watched and he watched.
But, in spite of his watch,
that bee didn't work any harder. Not mawtch.

So then somebody said,
"Our old bee-watching man
just isn't bee-watching as hard as he can.
He ought to be watched by *another* Hawtch-Hawtcher!
The thing that we need
is a Bee-Watcher-Watcher!"

WELL...

The Bee-Watcher-Watcher watched the Bee-Watcher.
He didn't watch well. So another Hawtch-Hawtcher
had to come in as a Watch-Watcher-Watcher!
And today all the Hawtchers who live in Hawtch-Hawtch
are watching on Watch-Watcher-Watchering-Watch,
Watch-Watching the Watcher who's watching that bee.
You're not a Hawtch-Watcher. You're lucky, you see!

And how fortunate *you're* not Professor de Breeze
who has spent the past thirty-two years, if you please,
trying to teach Irish ducks how to read Jivvanese.

And think of the
poor puffing Poogle-Horn Players,
who have to parade
down the Poogle-Horn Stairs
every morning to wake up
the Prince of Poo-Boken.
It's awful how often
their poogles get broken!

And, oh! Just suppose
you were poor Harry Haddow.
Try as he will.
he can't make any shadow!

He thinks that, perhaps, something's wrong with his Gizz.
And I think that, by golly, there probably is.

And the Brothers Ba-zoo.
The poor Brothers Ba-zoo!
Suppose *your* hair grew
like *theirs* happened to do!
You think *you're* unlucky...?
I'm telling you, Duckie,
some people are muchly,
oh, *ever* so muchly,
muchly more-more-more unlucky than you!

And suppose that you lived in that forest in France,
where the average young person just hasn't a chance
to escape from the perilous pants-eating-plants!
But *your* pants are safe! You're a fortunate guy.
And you ought to be shouting, "How lucky am I!"

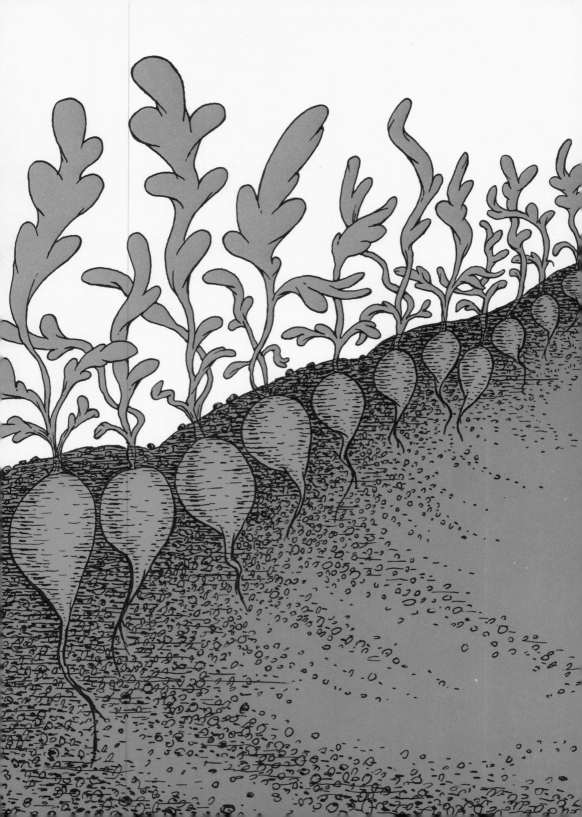

And, speaking of plants,
you should be greatly glad-ish
you're not Farmer Falkenberg's
seventeenth radish.

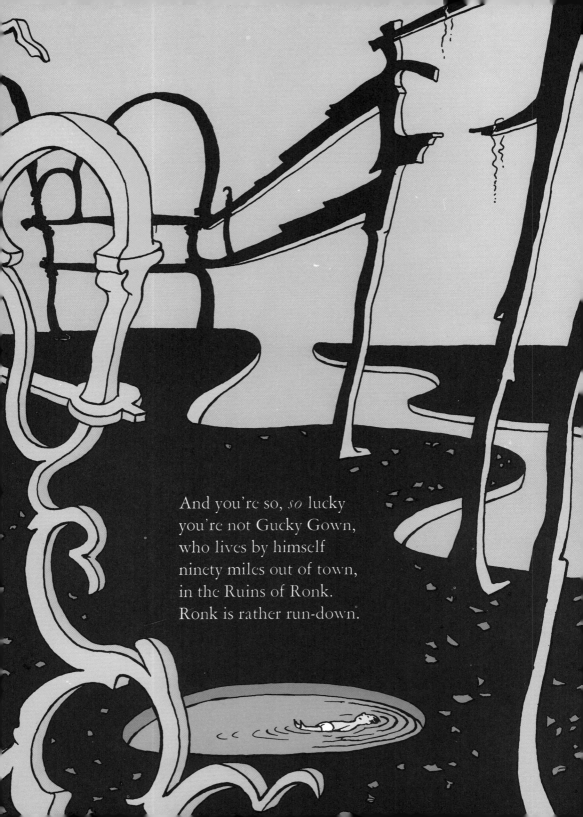

And you're so, *so* lucky
you're not Gucky Gown,
who lives by himself
ninety miles out of town,
in the Ruins of Ronk.
Ronk is rather run-down.

And you're so, *so, So* lucky
you're not a left sock,
left behind by mistake
in the Kaverns of Krock!

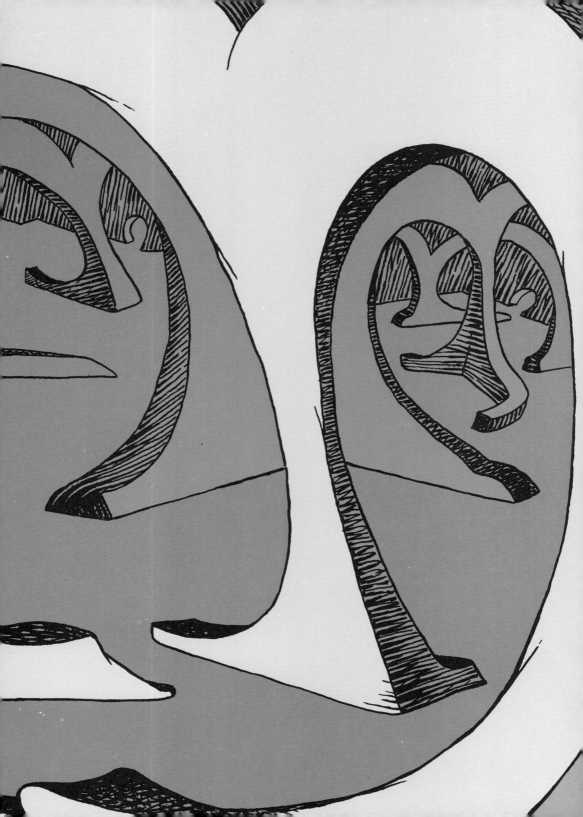

Thank goodness for all of the things you are not!
Thank goodness you're not something someone forgot,
and left all alone in some punkerish place
like a rusty tin coat hanger hanging in space.

That's why I say, "Duckie!
Don't grumble! Don't stew!
Some critters are much-much,
oh, ever so much-much,
so muchly much-much more unlucky than you!"

OTHER BOOKS BY DR. SEUSS

Yertle the Turtle

If I Ran the Circus

Thidwick: The Big-Hearted Moose

Horton Hatches the Egg

And to Think That I Saw It on Mulberry Street

The 500 Hats of Bartholomew Cubbins

How the Grinch Stole Christmas!

The Sneetches & Other Stories

Dr. Seuss's Sleep Book

I Had Trouble in Getting to Solla Sollew

The Cat in the Hat Song Book

I Can Lick 30 Tigers Today & Other Stories

The Lorax

Did I Ever Tell You How Lucky You Are?

AND FOR BEGINNING READERS

The Cat in the Hat

The Cat in the Hat Comes Back

One Fish Two Fish Red Fish Blue Fish

Green Eggs and Ham

Hop on Pop

Dr. Seuss's ABC

Fox in Socks

The Foot Book

My Book About Me, by Me, Myself

Mr. Brown Can Moo! Can You?

Marvin K. Mooney, Will You Please Go Now!

The Shape of Me and Other Stuff

The Many Mice of Mr. Brice

About

Dr. Seuss

Dr. Seuss really is a real person. His real name is Theodor Seuss Geisel, and that's what he was mostly known as, growing up in Springfield, Massachusetts, and through his years at Dartmouth and Oxford. He had always *planned* to be a teacher, but somehow he was always too busy doing funny drawings for various newspapers and magazines. But because someday he was going to be a serious teacher, he signed the funny drawings "Dr. Seuss."

Then in 1937 he wrote a children's book. At first no one would publish it, but finally someone did. And he signed *that* "Dr. Seuss." Luckily for children, Dr. Seuss has never had any more trouble getting his books published.

Not content with inventing marvelous new kinds of animals, Dr. Seuss decided to invent a marvelous new kind of book. In 1957 he wrote THE CAT IN THE HAT, and proved that even books for beginning readers could be fun. "The Cat" became the symbol for Beginner Books, a division of Random House, with Dr. Seuss as its president and editor-in-chief. He had become a teacher at last, showing millions of children the delights of learning to read.

Dr. Seuss lives in an old watchtower on top of a mountain in California, where he keeps busy writing, drawing, and working on a series of award-winning TV specials. Sometimes he comes down off the mountain to visit other mountains, or go to the dentist.

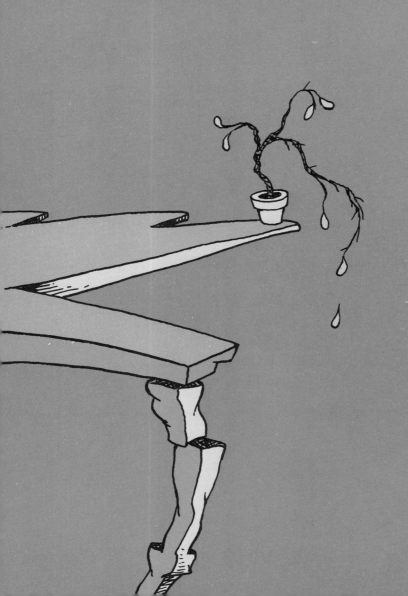